Science Projects for the Intermediate Grades

Science Projects
for the
Intermediate Grades

Maxine Springer Schneider
Consultant and Instructor of Science
Bellevue District, Kawana School
Santa Rosa, California

Fearon Teacher Aids
Carthage, Illinois

Dedicated to the boys and girls in the fifth and sixth grades at Kawana School in Santa Rosa, who tested the projects for a science fair, and to Lynn, Heather, and Meredith Gillis and Eric Nielson.

ISBN-0-8224-6310-5

Library of Congress Catalog Card Number: 70-132146

Printed in the United States of America.

Illustrated by Basil C. Wood

Contents

Introduction

The activities in this book are designed primarily for general use in the classroom, although they can be easily adapted for individual science projects. Most of the activities have been performed by students in the fifth and sixth grades for a science fair, and it has been found that these students have benefitted greatly by directly participating in science experiments.

The projects cover many topics, providing you with a large selection so that you may choose those projects that best fit the needs of your class. They are generally based on observation and thus are designed to help inform the teacher as well as the students.

To obtain the greatest benefit from these projects, it is suggested that they be treated in the same manner as experiments. In other words, the students should first discuss what they hope to gain from doing the project. Then everyone should become familiar with what is going to take place or how the experiment will be performed. When the project is completed, the students should draw conclusions as to what they have learned. In their discussion, they should decide whether or not they have gained the information they sought at the beginning of the project. If not, perhaps the experiment should be repeated or modified.

Some of the projects can be performed by a group of children; and it is suggested that, depending on the ability of the students, you assign these projects for a group presentation. In this way some of the burden is removed from you, and the children benefit by direct participation in science. You will also find that often a child can explain something to another child better than a teacher can.

Most of these projects use such easily-obtainable items as milk cartons, thread, and nails. For your electricity projects you will want to obtain a large amount of bell wire and at least one six-volt battery. It would probably be extremely useful to have a science cabinet where you can keep all your basic supplies for your science projects. In this way, your materials will always be readily available; and if you suddenly decide a point could be explained better by demonstration, you can use the materials from the cabinet rather than spending several days in gathering things together—and probably losing the class' interest in the interim.

This book provides the teacher, and in turn the class, with many good, basic science projects. It is hoped that creative minds will extend these projects, thus providing a greater depth of understanding. Encourage your children to perform these projects again at home and to change them as they so desire. You will find that by using projects and demonstrations, the interest of your students in science will grow and their general knowledge of science will improve.

CAUTION

This book is intended as a teacher's resource. Do not assign activities to students until you have instructed them in laboratory safety. Since even the simplest experiment done improperly may be dangerous, all general safety precautions should be taken. Be sure to allow for adequate ventilation and have a fire extinguisher readily available. Adult supervision should be maintained during any experiment.

Earth Sciences

Alum Crystals

Objective

To demonstrate the way in which crystals may be formed, and to examine alum crystals specifically.

Materials

A package of alum from the drugstore, a peanut butter jar and lid, a nail, a hammer, thread, boiling water, and tape.

Procedure

Punch a hole in the jar lid with the nail. Screw the lid on the jar and push the thread through the hole until the thread reaches the bottom. Anchor the other end by tying it to a nail, so it doesn't slip through the hole in the lid.

Boil enough water to fill your jar almost to the top. Place a cup of alum in the jar and then pour the water over it, leaving a small air space in the jar. Screw the lid back on, making sure the thread hangs free in the liquid. Tape the hole completely with masking tape.

Swish the water around by tipping the jar, shaking the alum up well. Repeat this action every fifteen minutes for a half hour. Wait an hour and then shake the jar again. Then set the jar in a quiet place where it will not be disturbed.

After an hour the crystals will begin to form, and by the next morning, you should have a whole string of crystals. Each time you do this experiment, you will find that your crystals will be different in size and overall appearance.

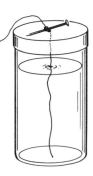

You might suggest that the students grow crystals at home, and then establish a day for them to bring their crystals to class for comparison. A magnifying glass will be extremely useful in helping them examine the basic structures of their crystals.

Erosion

Objective

To provide a classroom demonstration of erosion, and to draw conclusions as to the application of the demonstration to real situations.

Materials

An aquarium or large box, enough good soil mixed with sand to half fill your aquarium, hedge or plant clippings, and a sprinkling can or jar.

Procedure

Place the soil in your aquarium so that it forms a fairly steep slope. Make a flat surface at the top of the slope. Plant the clippings in this flat area, thus creating your hillside model. Ask the children if they know what will happen to the soil when it rains. Then sprinkle the clippings thoroughly each day.

Have the children make the following observations after they have studied the model:

1. When the water is running off the soil, where does the soil go?
2. How does the soil on the top look?
3. How does the soil on the bank look?
4. Is there new soil at the bottom of the tank? What does it look like?
5. What happens to the soil if little depressions are made around the clippings?
6. Japanese farmers plant their plants on little mounds of earth. This is called terracing. Try this and see what effect it has on the soil.
7. Have members of the class suggest other possible solutions to the erosion problem. Try implementing their suggestions on your model and observe whether their suggestions work.

Stalactites

Objective

To grow stalactites and demonstrate one way these formations may have grown naturally.

Materials

Two one-quart milk cartons, eighteen inches of string, Epsom salts, two small nails, and water.

Procedure

Cut the tops off the milk cartons and place fifteen teaspoons of Epsom salts and two cups of warm water in each carton. Mix the solution up well and soak the string in it. Tie a nail or any type of weight to each end of the string. Then hang one end of the string in each of the cartons, which should be placed about a foot apart. The nails help keep the string immersed in the solution.

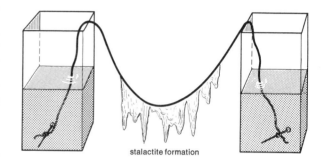
stalactite formation

Keep your cartons in a place that will not be disturbed. After a couple of weeks the stalactites should be forming on the string. If you have done an experiment on growing crystals, discuss the difference in formation times, shapes, and general appearances of crystals and stalactites.

Any absorbent material such as cord, yarn, etc., can be substituted for the string in this project. You might suggest that several children try this project at home using different materials, and then bring their stalactites to school for comparison.

Volcanoes

CAUTION: This experiment should be done outside. Stand back after lighting volcano.

Objective

To demonstrate the possible action of a volcano and its lava flow.

Materials

Ammonium dichromate, a large square board, wallpaper wheat paste, matches, and a small shallow can.

Procedure

Make a volcano shape on a board, using wallpaper wheat paste. Insert the small tin can in the top. Let the paste dry for a week; it will crack and form ridges. Apply another coat of

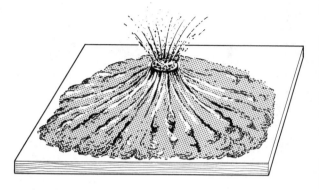

wheat paste to your volcano and let it dry again. Repeat this process, building up layers until you are satisfied with the shape of your volcano.

To make the volcano erupt, place at least ten kitchen match heads in the can and half fill the can with ammonium dichromate. Light a match and drop it into the mixture. It will get very hot, flare up, and give off sparks. A green substance will pour out over the volcano like lava. This may be repeated as often as you wish, but you may have to clean up the residue after each eruption.

Discuss the demonstration with your class, emphasizing the heat that is produced, the lava flow, its effect on the surrounding land, the way mountains may be built, and the way the model compares with a real volcano. Point out that there are many extinct volcanoes in the United States—Mt. Shasta in California, for example.

Growing Crystals

Objective
To show a way in which crystals may be formed.

Materials
A shallow pan, charcoal briquettes, 1/4 cup of salt, 1/4 cup of liquid bluing, 1/4 cup of water, three tablespoons of household ammonia, an eyedropper, food coloring, and a magnifying glass.

Procedure
Break the charcoal briquettes into small pieces and place them in a shallow pan. Pour the salt over the pieces, covering them well. Mix the ammonia, water, and bluing, and pour this mixture over the briquettes until they are saturated. Using an eyedropper, squeeze drops of food coloring on the pieces. Use several colors, so your crystals will be different colors. Allow the mixture to sit undisturbed overnight. The next day you should begin to see powdery crystals. These will continue to grow for several days.

Have the members of your class observe the crystals through a magnifying glass. These crystals are delicate and will not last very long if they are disturbed. The children should be able to examine the shape and the differences in color.

Preserving Fossils

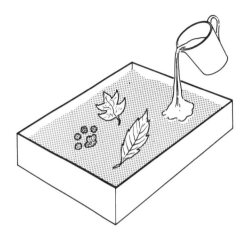

Objective
To show how fossils are preserved, and to discuss some of the physical characteristics of sedimentary rocks.

Materials
Cement, sand, lime, clay, water, a heavy cardboard box, and objects to be preserved.

Procedure
Mix equal parts of cement, lime, and sand. Add water to this mixture until it flows freely. This mixture is very similar to sandstone. If you wish, you may use plaster of Paris, but you will have to work quickly because it sets very fast.

Put a layer of clay in the bottom of a shallow cardboard box. Smooth the clay and then push the objects you wish to preserve into it until they form an impression. You may want to use shells, leaves, sticks, and feathers, for example. Remove the objects, and pour the mixture of cement, lime, sand, and water over the clay. Do not move the box until the mixture has hardened. When the mixture has set, remove the box and clay. Impressions of the fossils will be left in the sandstone.

Discuss with your class how sandstone may have been formed in nature and how nature removes the object that has left the impression.

This technique may also be used for making casts of animal tracks or for an interesting art project.

Dissolving Rocks

Objective
To demonstrate one way rocks are worn away in nature.

Materials
Sandstone, rocks, an old pan, and a weak acid such as vinegar.

Procedure
Place the sandstone in a pan and pour the acid over it. The acid will begin to fizz, and a gas will be liberated. The rock will begin to crumble and dissolve.

The sandstone is cemented sand and calcium carbonate. When the acid is added, a gas from the rock breaks free, causing the rock to dissolve.

Discuss the way acid is formed in nature and what effect this acid has on shaping mountains and rocks.

Sugar Crystals

Objective

To show how sugar crystals may be formed, and to examine their physical structure.

Materials

One pound of sugar, a quart of boiling water, a spoon, a quart jar, a sugar cube, and twelve inches of string.

Procedure

Pour one pound of sugar into the boiling water. Stir the mixture until all the sugar is dissolved. Let it cool and then pour the solution into a quart jar. Tie a sugar cube to the string and drop this into the cooled solution. After 36 hours sugar crystals should have formed on the string.

First have your class examine the structure of the crystals and then let them eat the crystals if they want.

2

Weather Sciences

A Rain Gauge

Objective

To build an instrument that will help you keep an accurate record of precipitation.

Materials

A large juice can, water, a narrow olive jar, marking pen, a ruler, a post, wire, nails and a hammer, a plastic funnel, masking tape.

Procedure

Remove the top from a juice can and pour water into the can until it is one inch deep. Pour the one inch of water into the olive jar. Mark the level of the water on the jar and label it one inch. Using a ruler and measuring from the bottom of the jar, divide this amount into ten equal parts. Mark the measurements on the side of the jar and then pour the water out. This olive jar is now a fairly accurate instrument for measuring rainfall in tenths of an inch increments.

To make your rain gauge, place the juice can on a platform on the post. Wrap the wire around the can and nail the wire to the post. Cut the plastic funnel so it fits the top of the can exactly and then tape it to the top of the can.

To use your rain gauge, place it outside in an upright position. After it has rained, pour the water from the can into the olive jar and measure it. If more than one inch falls, you will have to pour out the one inch in the jar before measuring the remaining water. You might have your class keep a total for the school year and record it on a graph.

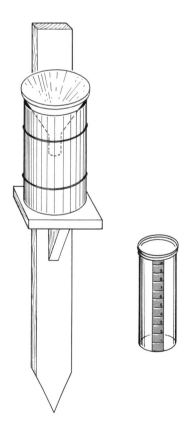

An Anemometer

Objective

To build an instrument that will enable you to measure the velocity of the wind.

Materials

A fifteen-inch square of wood, a three-foot-long 2 x 4 board, two slats three feet long by one inch wide, two large nails, a hammer, two small rubber balls cut in half, four long thumbtacks or brads, paint, a drill, and a washer.

Procedure

Nail the 2 x 4 board into the center of the square board, so that the 2 x 4 is upright. To the end of each three-foot-long slat, nail a rubber ball half so that it is facing the opposite direction from the one on the other end. Paint one of the four halves black and the other three any color other than black. When the paint has dried, you are ready to affix the slats to the upright. First, place the washer between the slats and the upright. Then nail the two slats through their edges and through the washer into the center of the upright 2 x 4. You may want to drill a hole in the top of the upright. Your anemometer should look like the illustration when you are finished.

To use your anemometer, count the number of times the black cup revolves in thirty seconds and divide by five. This figure will approximate the wind velocity.

Air Pressure

CAUTION: Always remove can from heat *before* sealing.

Objective

To demonstrate the effects of air pressure and condensation of water vapor.

Materials

An empty duplicating fluid can, water, a Bunsen burner or hot plate, potholders, and cold water.

Procedure

Clean the can out thoroughly and put an inch of water in it. Place it over the heat source and let the water boil for a minute or until steam is released. Seal the can tightly. Place the can under cold running water for thirty seconds. Then place the can so that your class can see it. As the cold water condenses the steam inside, a vacuum will be formed inside the can, and the air pressure on the outside will cause the can to be crushed.

Have your class decide what caused the can to collapse, and try to get them to relate this experiment to weather disturbances.

Atmospheric Pressure

Objective
To demonstrate the effects of atmospheric pressure, especially its relation to expansion and contraction.

Materials
An Erlenmeyer flask, a balloon, a Bunsen burner, and water.

Procedure
Place a small amount of water in the flask and heat it. As the water begins to boil, place a balloon over the top of the flask, making sure that the lip of the balloon is around the lip of the flask. The balloon will inflate. Remove the flask from the heat and let the water cool. As the water cools, the balloon will be drawn into the flask.

Have the class decide why the balloon inflated and then why it collapsed. They should decide that as the air condensed, it created a vacuum, and this, combined with the atmospheric pressure on the outside of the balloon, caused the balloon to be drawn into the flask.

A Barometer

Objective
To make an instrument that measures the change in air pressure.

Materials
A pint thermos bottle with matching cork stopper, a twelve-inch glass tube, glue, a wooden stand, wire, a quart jar lid, mineral oil, food coloring, a small box to fit around the thermos, newspaper, and a marking pen.

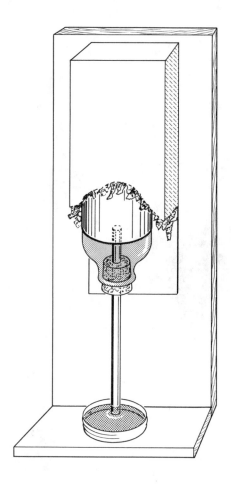

Procedure

Bore a hole into the cork and insert the glass tubing. Put the cork into the thermos and seal it tightly with glue. Invert the thermos and mount it on the wooden stand so that the tube will enter the quart jar lid by at least two-thirds of its depth. (The lid should be placed on the bottom of the stand prior to mounting the bottle.) Wire the thermos bottle to the stand so that it is secure. Place the cardboard box around the thermos and stuff the extra space with newspaper. If you don't insulate the thermos in this way, you would have a thermometer instead of a barometer. Fill the quart jar lid with mineral oil that has been dyed with food coloring. You now have your barometer.

The oil will rise up the tube until it finds a balance point. This point will indicate the barometric pressure for that day. You may want to mark this point, and then see how it compares with points on other days. As the air pressure goes up, the oil will rise; as it goes down, the oil will fall. You could try to calibrate your barometer by comparing the points with readings on a commercial barometer.

A Cloud Chamber

Objective

To build a cloud chamber in order to study how air condensation forms clouds.

Materials

A gallon jar with a lid, a black velvet cloth, rubbing alcohol, luminous paint, ice cubes, a large flat pan, and a flashlight.

Procedure

Saturate the velvet with rubbing alcohol and place the cloth inside the jar. Put some drops of paint on the cloth and screw the lid on the jar tightly. Set the jar on some ice cubes in the pan. As the jar gets colder, the alcohol will vaporize and condense. The luminous paint disintegrates and leaves trails. Condensation takes place along the trails. The jar must be very cold for this to happen.

Shine a light into the jar and have your class observe the vapor trails. Relate this condensation to the way in which clouds are formed.

Making Clouds

CAUTION: Inserting glass tubes into corks requires extreme care as the tube may snap or splinter.

Objective

To demonstrate how clouds are formed.

Materials

A clear bottle with a cork to seal it, a glass tube, grease, water, rubbing alcohol, and crushed chalk.

Procedures

Bore a hole in the cork and push the glass tubing through it. Rub the tube with grease or liquid detergent first to make it slide easier. Pour a mixture of alcohol and water into the bottle, wetting all sides of the bottle. Then pour this mixture out. Put a few pinches of crushed chalk into the bottle and cork it, making sure that it is tightly sealed. Blow through the tube until the chalk dust is flying around. Then suck out the air from the bottle using proper siphoning techniques. This should cause the air to expand and a cloud to be formed.

3 Plant Sciences

Growing Seeds Without Soil

Objective

To show how seeds may be grown without soil, and to illustrate the effect of this on the plant.

Materials

Several clear glasses, blotter paper or paper towels, cotton, water, and seeds.

Procedure

Line the inside of the glass with blotter paper or paper towels and fill the glass with cotton. Place some seeds (radish seeds grow very quickly) between the glass and the blotter or paper towel. Wet the cotton and make sure that it remains wet throughout the experiment.

You should be able to watch the seeds send out roots and leaves. Discuss the color and shape of the plant with your class, and have them determine the reasons for any unusual physical characteristics.

corn

radishes

beans

Growing Plants

Objective

To demonstrate a plant's need for sunshine.

Materials

Two potted plants of the same type and similar size.

Procedure

Place one plant in the sunshine and the other plant in a closet or other dark place. Make sure that both plants have the same advantages as far as watering and soil are concerned. It is important that your class understand that the only variant in this experiment is the sunshine. Observe the plants each day and have the children record what changes are taking place. After a while, it should become evident that the plant deprived of sunlight is suffering. The class should realize that this demonstrates the chemical change that occurs when light strikes the chlorophyll; the plant makes sugar by combining water and carbon dioxide.

Growing Mold

Objective

To grow one type of mold, and to discover its physical needs for growth.

Materials

Two slices of bread, jelly, a needle, paper plates, and a handful of sand.

Procedure

Place a slice of bread on a paper plate. Moisten the bread and put it in a warm place. In two or three days mold should appear on the bread. Put a fresh piece of bread on one paper plate and a pile of sand on another. Place some of the spores on the bread and some on the sand. Put these plates in a warm place and do not disturb them for a couple of days. Then let the class observe what has taken place. Add some jelly to the dry sand and leave the plates in the warm, secure spot. In a few days let the children observe the plates again. At this time, they should be able to draw some conclusions about this type of mold and the way it grows. Mold cannot produce its own food; it must live off other things.

Mold Comparison

Objective

To show how different molds can be formed and to discuss their differences.

Materials

Three quart jars with lids, a piece of fruit, a slice of bread, dead insects, and water.

Procedure

Place the piece of fruit and a little water in the first jar. Put a slice of bread that you have wiped over a dirty place and dampened slightly in the second jar. Place a few dead insects and a little water in the third jar. Screw the jar lids on tightly. Place the jars in a warm place for a week.

After a week has elapsed, show the jars to the class and have them discuss the differences among the molds. If you have used an orange for your fruit, point out that the green mold they see is penicillin and that it is very useful in curing infections.

Growing Bacteria

Objective

To grow bacteria in order to study their plant characteristics.

Materials

A slice of boiled potato and a flat dish with a lid.

Procedure

Place the potato in the dish and expose it to the air in a warm room. After several hours cover the dish and put it in a warm place where it will not be disturbed. A few days later have the class observe the potato. They should see several spots on the surface of it. These spots are colonies of bacteria. This bacteria is a harmless variety, but some bacteria can cause diseases. Have your class discuss where the bacteria came from and how this affects health and hygiene.

Trees and Wood

Objective

To provide a visual aid for students to help them in realizing the relationship between trees and their use.

Materials

A large varnished piece of plywood or a piece of heavy cardboard, chips of wood and bark from several types of trees, glue, pictures of these trees, a small history of each tree, some leaves from each tree, floor wax, and newsprint.

Procedure

Use the varnished plywood or the cardboard as the background for your display. You should select one type of tree to represent each of the five basic shapes—oval, square, oblong, triangular, and round. You might want to assign each shape to a committee of students and have them gather and prepare the necessary materials.

First, draw a picture or provide a photograph of each type of tree selected and mount these across the top of the display board. Visit a lumberyard to obtain a scrap of wood for each tree that has been selected. Glue the wood scraps below the tree pictures.

Then research the history of each tree and prepare a written description of its physical characteristics and uses. Paste these descriptions under the appropriate tree.

If you want to include leaves from each tree, dip them in liquid floor wax, dry them between newsprint, and mount them on the display board.

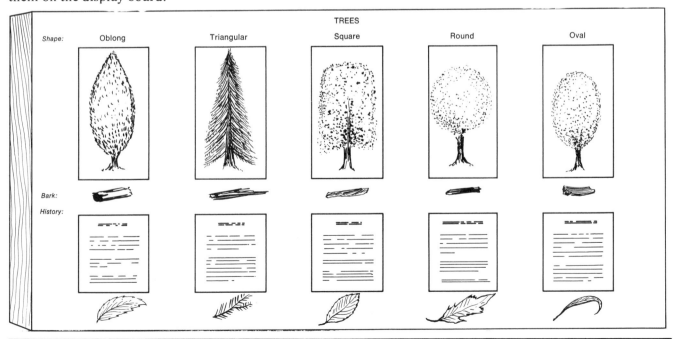

Nature Printing

Objective

To use plants in art, thus helping the children to learn about different types of plants and their individual beauty.

Materials

Two pieces of 18" x 11" construction paper, scissors, crayons, waxed paper, glue, and an iron.

Procedure

Have each child arrange leaves, weeds, or any other plant life that appeals to him on a light piece of construction paper. Using scissors, he should shave some different colored crayons over and around his plant life. The shavings should be small. Over this, place a piece of waxed paper equal in size to the construction paper. Have the child carefully carry his picture to you. With the iron on the next to the lowest heat, press the picture, moving slowly from one side to the next. This should weld the picture together. Have the child take his picture back to his desk and make a border for it from the other piece of construction paper. The border should be glued down and the names of his plants written very lightly on the back of the picture.

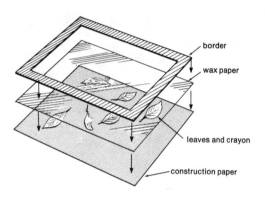

border

wax paper

leaves and crayon

construction paper

Spatterprinting

Objective

To study the different shapes of small leaves and plants.

Materials

Several rectangles of wire screening, an old toothbrush for each color of paint, poster paint, leaves and plants, masking tape, and construction paper.

Procedure

Wrap the edges of the screens with tape so the children will not hurt themselves on the sharp wires. You should have one screen for each color. You might also want to make wooden frames and nail the screening to them. The wooden frame can be placed directly over the paper so the child doesn't have to hold the screen while spattering the paint.

Have the children choose the leaves and plants they want to print, the paper they want to print them on, and the color of paint they want to use. They should arrange the leaves or plants on the construction paper in any way that pleases them. Then, holding the screen over their arrangement, they should move a toothbrush that has been dipped in paint back and forth over the screen to make spatters. The paint should not be thin. When the paint has dried, the children should remove their leaves or plants. Have them write the names of the leaves or plants on their print, and then display all the prints so the children can learn to identify leaves and plants.

Osmosis

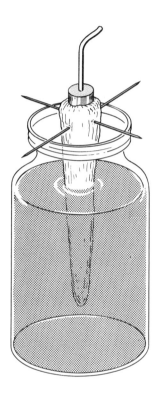

Objective
To demonstrate how water rises in plants.

Materials
A large carrot, a quart jar, a carrot peeler, a knife, a small cork or rubber stopper, syrup, two feet of glass tubing, glue, and four toothpicks.

Procedure
Peel the carrot. Cut a hole in the top center portion of the carrot to fit the cork. Using the peeler, make this hole about two to three inches deep. Place syrup in the hole, leaving room for the stopper. Make a hole in the center of the stopper, and push the glass tubing through it. Put the stopper into the hole in the carrot and glue it so that it is airtight. Stick four tooth-picks into the sides of the carrot near the top. Fill the jar with water and suspend the carrot in it.

The water should move through the carrot and up the tube. This is because osmosis causes the water (a low concentration) to move through the carrot faster than syrup (a high concentration) can move out.

Capillary Action

Objective
To demonstrate the physical characteristics of osmosis and capillary action.

Materials

A few stalks of celery, three small glasses, food coloring, a knife, and possibly a microscope.

Procedure

Place a stalk of celery in a glass of water that has been dyed with blue food coloring. After a few hours you should be able to see the food coloring moving up the stalk; by the next morning, it will have reached the top. Try the experiment again, but this time split one end of the stalk into thirds. Color three glasses of water with a different food coloring. Place each part of the stalk in a different glass. Let the color flow to the top of the piece of celery and observe what happens. If you can, examine the stems under a microscope.

This movement of water up the stem is called capillary action; in roots and trees it is called osmosis.

Animal Sciences

Making an Incubator

Objective

To build an incubator, and to incubate and hatch some chicken eggs.

Materials

A heavy cardboard box with a lid, a sheet of glass smaller than the side of the box, masking tape, a sixty-watt light bulb, a socket with a plug-in cord, a thermometer, a small pan of water, and a number of fertilized chicken eggs (you can get these from a poultry supply house).

Procedure

Cut a hole in the side of the cardboard box slightly smaller than your piece of glass. Tape the glass in the box so that it covers the hole. The edges should be sealed so no air can escape. Wire the lightbulb socket into the back of the box (opposite the window). Tape the holes so the box is airtight. Affix a thermometer to the back so that it can be seen through the window. Now you are ready to put the eggs in. Place the eggs on the bottom of the box with a pan of water beside them to keep the air moist. Put a sixty-watt lightbulb in the socket and plug the socket in. This will keep the temperature between 103° and 104°. Place the lid on the box. It should fit as tightly as possible, but don't seal it, because you will have to get into the box every day.

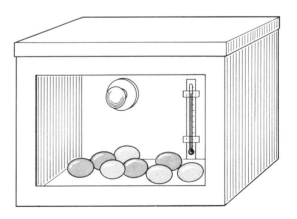

Each day you should check the temperature to make sure it is within the proper limits. If the temperature is too low, the lid is not tight and air is entering. You may also need a higher watt bulb. If the temperature is too high, use a lower watt bulb.

You will have to turn the eggs at least once each day, but not more than twice. This turning action keeps the baby chicks from being deformed by having their heads or feet stick to the shell. You may sprinkle water over them periodically. The eggs should hatch in 22 days.

Collecting Specimens

Objective

To provide a standard method of collecting and displaying animal specimens.

Materials

Denatured alcohol, jars, specimens, aluminum paint, and labels.

Procedure

Place your specimens in jars that are appropriate for their size, one specimen per jar. Arrange them nicely, so they can be clearly seen. Suggested specimens include frogs, bird eggs, small fish, mice, moles, lizards, and snakes. Pour the alcohol into the jar until it covers the specimen. This should keep your specimen preserved for about two years. If at any time the alcohol is below the specimen, put more alcohol in the jar. Screw the lids on your specimen jars. For uniformity, paint the lids with aluminum paint and label each jar. The label should tell what the specimen is and where and when it was found. Make sure the label does not obstruct the view of the specimen.

An Ant Village

Objective

To see how ants work and live.

Materials

An aquarium with a glass lid or a closed cardboard box with a glass window, ants, tape, dark paper, sugar water, and a sponge.

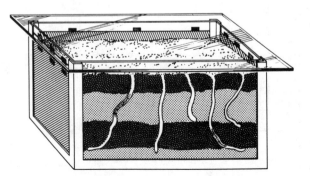

Procedure

Look for an anthill. When you have found one, dig it up, taking the queen ant (she is larger than the other ants), as many of the other ants as you can get, and the dirt from their hill. Place all this in your aquarium. Cover the top and tape it *tightly shut* so the ants can't get out. For at least one week keep the ants in a dark place. This will give them time to repair their village. Each day you will have to put a moist sponge in the tank to keep the soil from drying out. To feed the ants, you should place some sugar water or honey in the box. After a week, display the ants for your class to watch. You should probably cover three of the sides of the tank with dark paper. Allow your class a week or so to observe the ants and then have a discussion on how the ants live.

Seashells

Objective

To display shells attractively for observation and comparison.

Materials

Thin plywood boards, shells, paint, yarn, thin cardboard, and glue; and/or plaster of Paris, a wooden frame, sand, shells, and plastic spray.

Procedure

1. Plywood display—Cut the plywood in any shape you desire and paint it. Glue yarn to the top for a hanger. Cut cardboard rectangles, paint them, and glue them to the plywood. Then glue your shells to them. Write the name of the shells in small letters next to them. You now have an attractive display for your shell collection. Allow the children several days to look at the shells, and then discuss the differences and similarities.
2. Plaster of Paris display—Place freshly mixed plaster of Paris in a thin layer in a rectangular wooden frame. Cover this area quickly with clean sand. Scratch the shape of the object you would like to make in the sand—a fish, for example. Fill this area in with small seashells, overlapping them as you progress. Use liquid cement. You can also add other sea life such as seaweed, small crabs, sand dollars, and coral. Paint the frame of your display and spray the display with clear plastic spray.

    This project is best combined with a field trip to the seashore, if possible.

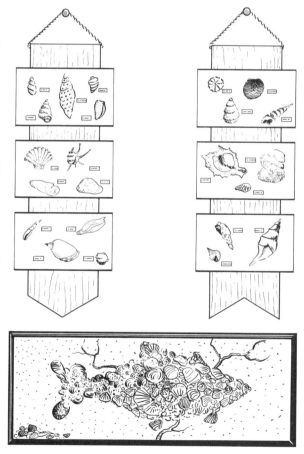

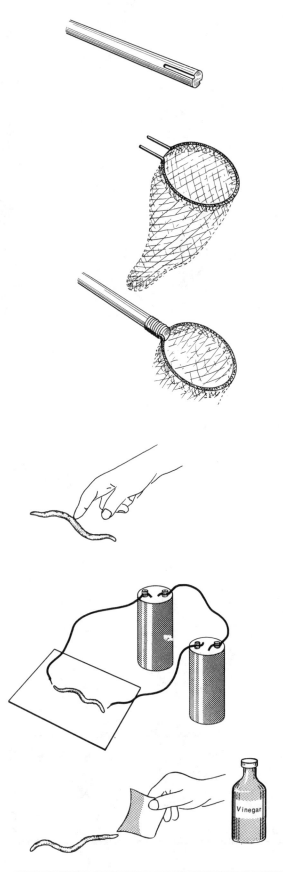

Butterfly Nets

Objective
To make a butterfly net or fish net for collection purposes.

Materials
A wire coat hanger, wire cutters, a mop or broom handle, a saw, tape, a needle, thread, and netting or old sheets.

Procedure
Bend the wire coat hanger until it is in the shape of a hoop. Cut the hook off. The two ends of the wire should be parallel. Saw two slots on the end of a broom handle and force the ends of the coat hanger into the slots. Tape the wires to the handle firmly. Cut the netting for a butterfly net in a triangle. The base should be large enough to fit around the loop and the length should be twelve inches. For a fish net, cut two rectangles nine inches long and as wide as one half the loop and a circle the size of the loop for the bottom. Sew up the pieces and sew them around the hoop.

It takes practice to learn how to use the net to catch insects. You have to wave it with a sweeping motion.

Worm Reactions

Objective
To test a worm's reactions to various stimuli.

Materials
Worms, paper, dry cell batteries, wire, vinegar, ammonia, ice, and cloth.

Procedure
Set up your dry cell batteries with one wire for each charge. Lay a worm on a piece of paper. With the class gathered around the demonstration area, touch the ends of the wires to the worm. Have the children respond to the worm's reaction. Push the worm with your finger and observe the reaction. Have the children comment on this and other stimuli, such as a cloth saturated with vinegar, a drop of ammonia on the worm's back, and ice.

Prehistory Diorama

Objective

To provide a semirealistic view of prehistory.

Materials

A large cardboard carton (the size paper towels come in), a plywood or cardboard tray to fit the box, nails, wooden slats, dirt or sand, tagboard, a light, paints, a dish, water, oil, and models of trees and dinosaurs.

Procedure

Remove one of the longer sides from the carton. This should be the back of the box. Paint the inside of the box a dark color. Slide a tray filled with dirt into the box. (The tray is useful for keeping the dirt in place while arranging the scene, although it is not absolutely essential to have a tray.) Nail the slats to the tray or box. Fill a dish with water and oil and place it in the dirt to resemble a tar pit. Arrange the models in a realistic manner. (The models can be made from clay, papier-mâche, etc., or purchased at a dime store.) On the tagboard, paint a volcano using lots of red, yellow, and orange, and attach it to the slats so that it faces what will be the front of the box. Cut a hole in the front of the carton so the children can look in on the scene. Place the light at the back of the diorama to make the volcano glow.

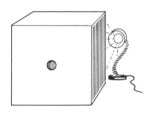

5

Human Sciences

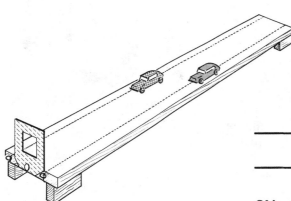

Depth Perception

Objective
To build an instrument that will test depth perception.

Materials
A board 8" x 6', four small eyescrews, string, two small cars, a piece of thin cardboard, and a thumbtack.

Procedure
Screw two eyescrews into the ends of the board. Thread string through the eyescrew on one end and the corresponding eyescrew on the other end. Tie the string together so you can pull it around. Do the same with the other eyescrews. Tie a car to each string so you can pull it either forward or backward.

Cut a small square opening in the cardboard and thumbtack it to the front end of the board.

To use this instrument to test perception, close one eye and try to line the cars up by moving the strings. Try using both eyes to line the cars up and see how much easier it is. Some people cannot see depths using both eyes.

Optical Illusions

Objective

To demonstrate that you cannot always trust your eyes.

Materials

Copies of the illustration for each child.

Procedure

Make a copy of the art for each child. You may also want to make other pictures for them, such as tail on a horse, boy on a bicycle, cat on a branch of a tree, etc. Have them hold the picture about an arm's length from their eyes and stare at the dot in the middle of the picture. They should slowly bring the picture toward their faces. The face in the picture should suddenly appear on the pumpkin. This is an optical illusion.

Lung Models

Objective

To demonstrate how the lungs work.

Materials

A milk carton, a knife, glue, masking tape, a nail, two soda straws, balloons, string, and plastic wrap; and/or a gallon jug, tape, a glass cutter, a one-hole rubber stopper, a glass y tube, an inner tube or rubber sheeting, and a large rubber band.

Procedure

1. Milk carton model—Cut a window in one side of the milk carton. Glue or tape the spout end shut tightly. Using a nail, punch two holes side-by-side in the bottom of the carton and push a soda straw through each hole. Reach through the window and tie a balloon around each straw. Adjust the straws so the balloons appear in the window. Glue plastic wrap over the window. To make the model work, squeeze the sides in. The balloons inflate with pressure and deflate when you let go.

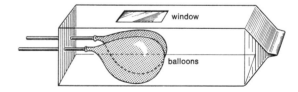

2. Gallon jug model—cut the bottom off the jug and tape the edges so you won't cut yourself. (You can have this done at a glass shop for a small charge.) Put the stopper in the jug. Push the ends of the y tube through the hole in the bottom of the rubber stopper and put a small balloon on each of

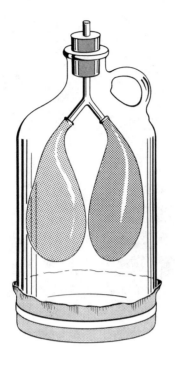

the other ends. Stretch the rubber sheeting over the bottom of the jug and use the rubber band to keep it tight.

Pushing your fist into the rubber diaphragm and pulling it back stimulates the human diaphragm. The action of the balloons depicts what happens to the lungs as the diaphragm works.

A Stethoscope

Objective

To examine the way the human heart beats by using a stethoscope.

Materials

Rubber tubing, three small funnels, and a y tube.

Procedure

Cut the rubber tubing into three pieces and insert a funnel into one end of each piece. Push the rubber tubings onto each branch of the y tube. You now have a stethoscope.

Have the children listen to their heartbeat by holding two of the funnels to their ears and the other to their hearts. They should be able to recognize a pattern to the beating.

Your Beating Pulse

Objective

To observe the human pulse.

Materials

A thumbtack and a toothpick or a small strip of balsa wood for each child.

Procedure

Have each child push the thumbtack into the wood and place the head of the thumbtack on the spot on his wrist where he can feel his pulse beating. He should be able to feel his pulse with his fingers; make sure he doesn't use his thumb. The piece of wood should bobble with every beat of the pulse. Each child can obtain his pulse rate by counting the number of beats per minute.

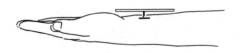

Fingerprinting

Objective

To demonstrate how fingerprints differ.

Materials

An inked stamp pad, a sheet of paper for each child, and a pen for each child.

Procedure

Fingerprint each child in your class by pressing each finger on the ink pad using a side-to-side rolling motion. Then press each finger on a sheet of paper, using the same rolling motion. Have the child write his name on the paper.

Display all the fingerprints so the children can compare them. They should conclude that no two people have the same fingerprints.

6

Electrical Sciences

A Galvanometer

Objective

To build an instrument that will detect the presence of an electric current and show the direction of the current.

Materials

Twenty to thirty feet of bell wire, a glass or bottle, a thin nail, thread, a dry cell, and a magnet.

Procedure

Tightly wrap the wire around your bottle, leaving a foot of wire hanging from each end. Magnetize a thin nail by stroking the ends of the nail with a magnet. Stroke them in opposite directions so you can obtain two poles. Then using the thread, hang this nail from the top of your wire coil, allowing it to hang freely in the opening. Lay the coil so the open ends are facing north and south. This is your galvanometer.

To test your galvanometer, attach the loose wires to the dry cell. If there is a current present, the nail should swing parallel to the coil of wire.

A galvanometer can be used to test small amounts of current. It can detect an amount so small that it would not even light a lightbulb. If you mark the directions of the magnetic field on your nail, you can also determine the direction of flow. You can demonstrate alternating current by switching the attached wires to the opposite poles. When you do this, your nail should swing around and point in the opposite direction.

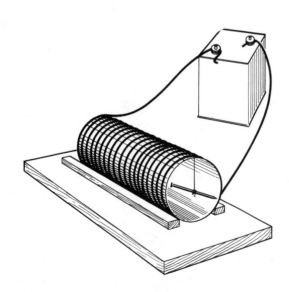

An Electroscope

Objective

To demonstrate the electrical charges of various objects.

Materials

Fur, a piece of paper, a plastic comb, and a ruler; and/or a gallon jug, a cork, a stiff piece of wire, and a small piece of foil.

Procedure

1. Ruler—Fold a piece of paper over a ruler and rub it very hard with a piece of fur. When you lift the ruler up, the sides of the paper should fly apart. This is caused by the like charges you have put on the paper. Rub a plastic comb with the fur and hold it in between the leaves of paper. Ask your class to comment on what happens and why it happens.

2. Gallon jug—Push a heavy wire through the cork stopper of the jug. Bend the wire so that a hook is formed and place a piece of aluminum foil over it. Lower the wire into the bottle until you can cork the jug. Rub a comb with a piece of fur and hold it next to the wire that is protruding from the top of the jug. Have the class comment on what happens and why it happens. Take other familiar items, rub them with fur, and place them near the wire to see what effect they have on the foil.

   The foil reacts to the type of charge in the item brought near the wire. If there is no reaction, the item does not have a noticeable charge.

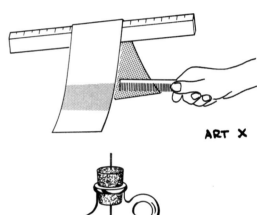

ART X

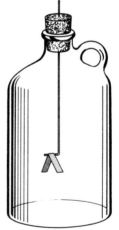

Testing Electricity

Objective

To test common objects for possible electric charges.

Materials

A lucite rod, a square of wool, and various substances such as a wool pad, flour, sand, sawdust, pith balls, thread, shredded paper, and iron filings.

Procedure

Very firmly and vigorously rub a lucite rod with wool cloth. While you are rubbing the rod, have some children place samples of the items to be tested on a table. Have the children watch as you bring the rod close to one item at a time. If necessary, rub the rod some more between each test. Have the members of your class comment upon the electrical charges of the items they have tested. See if they can make any generalizations about electrical charges of different types of materials.

A Lemon Battery

Objective
To demonstrate a property of an electric cell and the need of an electrolyte for current.

Materials
A citrus fruit, a strip of zinc, and a strip of copper.

Procedure
Roll your lemon or other fruit until it is very juicy. Push the strips of metal into the lemon about a half inch apart. Have a member of your class put his tongue between the two metals so that they touch his tongue simultaneously. Have him describe what he felt. If you can make several of these cells, you should have several children explain what they feel. Have the class decide what has caused this sensation. They should decide that the lemon juice has acted as an electrolyte conducting a current between the two metals. If you have an instrument to test very low voltages, you can measure the charge that is produced by your battery.

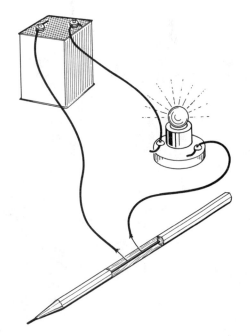

A Rheostat

Objective
To build an instrument that will graphically illustrate the principle that as resistance increases, current decreases—a rheostat.

Materials
A lead pencil, a knife, a small light bulb and socket, two short lengths of wire, and a battery.

Procedure

Cut the wood away from a lead pencil until you have exposed about two inches of the lead. Connect one side of the miniature socket with its bulb to one pole of the battery and attach a length of wire to the other side of the socket. Attach another length of wire to the other pole of the battery. Strip the ends of the loose wires so that they are no longer insulated. Press the two exposed ends to the lead. If the ends are close together, the bulb will light. As the distance between the ends is increased, the light intensity decreases. Have your children decide why this happens. They should determine that lead is a very poor conductor, a resistor, and as the resistance is increased, the current decreases.

Magnetic Fields

Objective

To demonstrate the extent and properties of a magnetic field exerted by a horseshoe magnet.

Materials

Thread, a heavy horseshoe magnet, paper clips, and a pencil.

Procedure

Hang the horseshoe magnet over a bar, such as the back of a chair. Tie lengths of thread to several paper clips and give one to each of several children. Have them hold the top of their thread and slowly bring the paper clip near the magnet until the thread is bent but the paper clip is not stuck to the magnet. When all the paper clips are attracted, pass a pencil between the clips and the magnet to demonstrate that the field will not be broken.

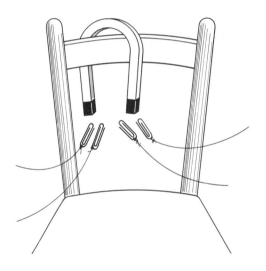

An Electromagnet

Objective

To demonstrate how field strength of an electromagnet varies with the number of coils.

Materials

Several two-penny nails or spikes, three feet of bell wire, and a six-volt battery.

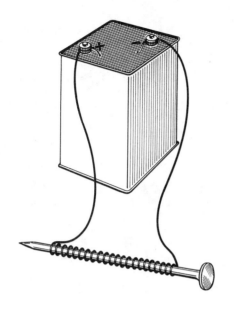

Procedure

Wrap a piece of bell wire tightly around a nail, allowing the ends to hang free. Connect the ends to the battery and you have now created an electromagnet. When the wires are disconnected, the nail is no longer magnetized. Wrap several other nails with wire, varying the amount of coils on each. Test if there is a difference in the magnetic strength of the nails in proportion to the number of coils by determining the pulling force of each nail. You can have a child measure the distance over which a magnet has effect and record it along with the number of coils for that magnet.

When all the results have been recorded, have the class discuss them and determine any general statement that can be applied to all electromagnets. You might also try reversing the pole designations of a particular magnet by reversing the battery attachments.

Finding Magnetic Fields

Objective

To discover the magnetic property of an electric field.

Materials

A six-volt battery, three feet of bell wire, dowels, tagboard, a square of plywood, a switch, and iron filings.

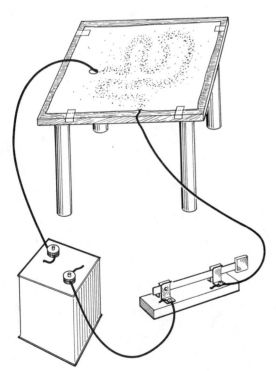

Procedure

Build a small table using dowels for the legs and plywood for the top. Connect a switch to a battery so that it makes a complete circuit. Strip the insulation from the middle of one of the wires and place the stripped portion on the table in any pattern you want. Place a piece of tagboard over the wire on top of the table and sprinkle iron filings onto the tagboard. Tape the edges of the tagboard to the table. Turn the switch on and the filings should line up in the same pattern as the wire beneath the tagboard. Have the members of your class discuss why the filings did this.

7

Chemical Sciences

Distilling Water

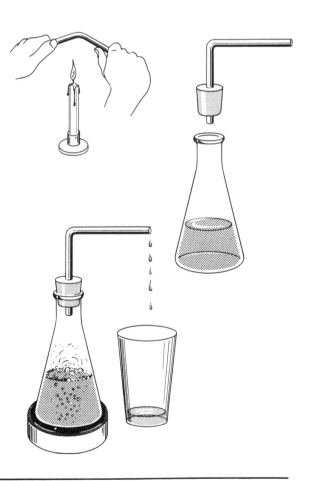

Objective

To distill a liquid and thereby demonstrate a chemical property of water.

Materials

A glass, glass tubing, a candle, a one-hole rubber stopper, an Erlenmeyer flask, food coloring, and a Bunsen burner or hot plate.

Procedure

Hold a piece of glass tubing over a candle flame until you can bend it to form a right angle. One side should be longer than the other. Put the tubing through the stopper, leaving the longer end hanging out. Pour water into the flask and add a few drops of food coloring. Put the cork and tubing into the flask and place it over the heat source. Place the glass under the end of the tubing, so it will collect the water as it drips. The water should boil, evaporate, and condense, leaving the impurities (food coloring) in the flask. Have a member of your class explain what is happening.

Testing for Acids and Bases

Objective

To execute a standard chemical test—test for acid or base.

Materials

Test tubes, Epsom salts, water, egg white, baking soda, and lemon juice.

Procedure

1. Base—Place a teaspoon of Epsom salts in a test tube. Dissolve the salts with water and add a few drops of ammonia. A white precipitate will form, which indicates the presence of a base.
2. Acid—Place some baking powder in a test tube and add a teaspoon of egg white. Then add a few drops of lemon juice. The mixture should begin to bubble, releasing CO_2 gas. This action indicates the presence of an acid.

Have your class discuss the difference between the two reactions and what this might indicate about the general nature of acids and bases.

Making CO_2

Objective

To create a gas by a chemical reaction, and to demonstrate some of the properties of CO_2.

Materials

Vinegar, baking soda, measuring spoons, measuring cup, a glass, a pill bottle with a plastic push-on cap, a match, and a baking pan.

Procedure

Put two tablespoons of baking soda into a glass. Pour one-third cup of vinegar quickly into the glass. The glass should be placed in a baking pan so that the bubbles will be caught in the pan as they spill over the top of the glass. The bubbles are formed by the CO_2 gas that is produced from the reaction.

To test some of the powers of CO_2, put some baking soda into a pill bottle and add vinegar. Quickly push the cap onto the bottle and set it on the table. As the pressure builds up, the cap should fly off. (Do not use a bottle with a screw-on cap because the experiment won't work.) To make sure that you have produced CO_2, light a match and hold it next to the bubbles. It should go out. Have your class discuss why the flame went out and describe the general aspects of CO_2 gas.

A CO_2 Boat

Objective

To demonstrate a property of carbon dioxide.

Materials

A metal powder can (tooth powder or talcum powder, etc.), plywood, tape, hammer and nails, vinegar, bicarbonate of soda, and a large dishpan.

Procedure

The plywood should be larger than the can and should be pointed on one end. Attach the can so that the top of the can is at the pointed end of the board. With the nail and hammer, punch a hole in the the bottom of the can. Fill the can two-thirds full with bicarbonate of soda and pour in some vinegar. Quickly cap the can and place it in a large pan of water, board side down. It should zoom around the pan on the top of the water.

Have members of your class tell why they think this happened. They should say that the gas formed by the vinegar and soda (CO_2) escapes out the back, and the opposite force of the escaping gas projects the boat forward.

A CO_2 Rocket

CAUTION: This experiment should be done only by adults.

Objective

To demonstrate the power of released CO_2 gas.

Materials

Tagboard, a rubber stopper, glue, CO_2 cartridge, paper clips, tape, a nail, a hammer, and twenty feet of fishing line.

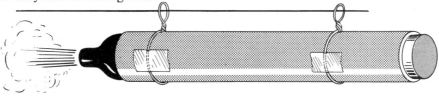

Procedure

Roll a 9" x 12" piece of tagboard around a CO_2 cartridge. Tape it to the cartridge and glue the stopper in the other end. This unit should be airtight. Wrap a couple of paper clips around the unit so they will form hooks. Tape the clips down. Thread the fishing line through the hooks and tie the ends to two objects twenty feet apart and a few feet above the ground. Holding the unit firmly at one end of the fishing line, knock a hole in the CO_2 cartridge with a hammer and nail. Quickly release the rocket, and it will shoot along the line giving off a white smoke.

Have your class discuss how powerful they think the release of the gas is, and then test the theories by seeing how far the cartridge will go.

A Model of an Atomic Element

Objective

To provide students with a three-dimensional model of an atom.

Materials

Baling wire, a three-foot-long dowel, tagboard, a 2" x 4" x 4" board, rubber cement, a drill, tape, and a styrofoam ball for each electron in the atom.

Procedure

Drill a hole in the board and glue the dowel into it. Form a circle of baling wire for each electron shell that you need. (An atomic element chart will tell you how many shells are needed for each element.) Tape these circles at the top and bottom of the dowel. Cut each styrofoam ball in half and glue it around the wire, making sure that you glue the specified number to each shell. In the center of the post glue a circle of tagboard that has the nucleus description written on it. Glue a display card that tells the type of atom, the shell description, and the arrangement of the electrons, neutrons, and protons to the bottom of the model.

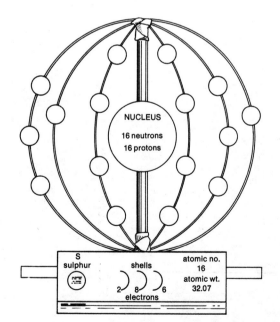

8

General Physical Sciences

A Planet Mobile

Objective

To provide a model of the solar system illustrating relative sizes of the planets, their colors, and their distances from the sun.

Materials

A 1" x 12" x 5' board, two 2 x 4 boards four feet long, a five-foot-long 1/2-inch dowel, a styrofoam ball for each planet, thumbtacks, a large piece of orange poster board, a small piece of white poster board, paint, thread, crayons, a hammer, and several large nails.

Procedure

Nail the 2 x 4 boards upright on the ends of the large board; cut slits in the top of the uprights and place the dowel in the slits. Cut a large circle from the orange poster board and thumbtack it on the left post to represent the sun. Daub brown paint spots and streaks on the sun to represent sunspots and storms. Paint each styrofoam ball to match a planet; try to make the balls the appropriate relative size. Cut a circle of white poster board. Color the circle with the rings that designate Saturn. Cut a hole in the middle of the tagboard and fit it over the planet painted to represent Saturn. Attach a thread to each planet and hang it from the sun at the appropriate relative distance. On the opposite post, hang a chart of information concerning the solar system.

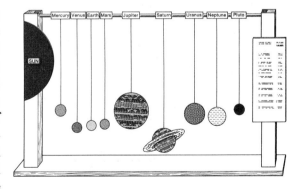

A Compass

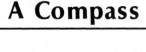

Objective

To make a compass that will demonstrate the magnetic fields of the Earth.

Materials

A saucer, talcum powder, a needle, a magnet, a cork, and a knife; and/or a magnet, a needle, paper, thread, and a bottle with a cork.

Procedure

1. Dish—Fill a saucer with water and sprinkle talcum powder over it. Magnetize a needle by stroking one end of the needle over one end of the magnet. Then do the same thing with the other end of the needle and the magnet. Stick the needle through the top of a cork and float the cork in the water. The needle should point in a north-south direction. Determine which end is north and which end is south.

2. Bottle—Magnetize a needle as explained above and stick it through a folded piece of paper. Attach one end of the thread to the paper and the other end to the bottle cork. Place the cork in the bottle, making sure the thread hangs free. The needle should settle in a north-south direction.

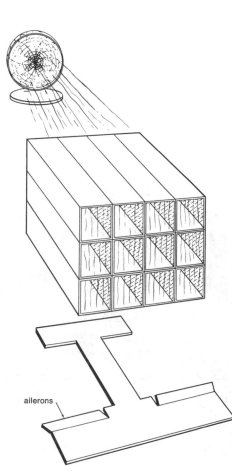

ailerons

A Wind Tunnel

Objective

To study the effects of wind and how airplanes adjust to these effects.

Materials

Twelve empty milk cartons, tape, a knife, glue, thread, an electric fan, and tagboard.

Procedure

Cut the ends off the milk cartons and stack them in a three by four array. Tape them together and glue small pieces of thread from the openings on the front. Allow the fan to blow through the cartons and observe the movement of the threads. Position the fan in different spots and see if the effect changes.

Make an airplane from tagboard as shown in the illustration. Crease one aileron up and the other down. Attach a thread to the plane, hold it in front of the cartons, and turn the fan on. Have the class observe what happens. Reverse the ailerons and again observe what happens. Try the airplane with the ailerons level, with them both up, and with them both down. After you have tried all possible combinations, have members of the class tell how they think airplanes are directed.

A Thermometer

Objective
To study the air temperature by means of a thermometer.

Materials
A pop bottle, clay, water, food coloring, and a soda straw.

Procedure
Fill the bottle two-thirds full of water and dye it with food coloring. Squeeze clay around the middle of a soda straw and put it into the bottle, using the clay to cap the bottle. Mark the level of the water and place the bottle in the sun for a short period of time. Observe if there has been any change in the level of the water, and have your class comment on why the change took place. Repeat the experiment, placing the bottle in a cool place.

A Steam Turbine

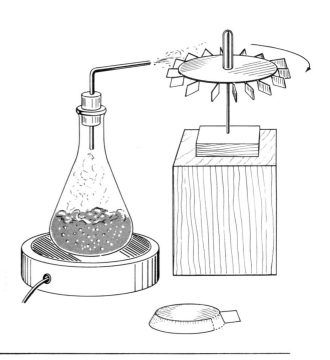

Objective
To show how steam can be used to perform mechanical work.

Materials
An aluminum pie tin, a hammer, a spike, a four-inch square of wood, a small board, a test tube, glass tubing, a one-hole rubber stopper, an Erlenmeyer flask, water, and a hot plate.

Procedure
Cut half-inch slits around the edge of a pie tin about one-fourth of an inch apart. Twist the slices so they stand out as blades. Nail a spike through the center of the small board. Put the small board on the wood block. Cut a hole in the pie tin large enough to fit over the test tube, but small enough so that

it will hang on the lip of the test tube without slipping off. Place it on the test tube and place the test tube over the spike. (If the test tube is too long, you may have to cut it down and glue the pie pan to it.) This is the turbine portion of your model. To make the steam, place a flask with water in it on the hot plate. Insert a bent piece of glass tubing in the stopper and put the stopper in the flask. Turn the tubing toward the turbine. As the water begins to boil and produces steam, the turbine should begin to turn around. When the system is operating effectively, discuss with your class exactly what is happening and have them suggest possible uses for this power.

A Balance Scale

Objective

To make a scale for studying comparative weights of objects.

Materials

A wooden coat hanger, two wooden clothespins, two small nails, a hammer, two paper cups, and materials to be weighed.

Procedure

Clip a clothespin to each end of a hanger, adjusting them until the hanger balances. Once you establish the position of the clothespins needed to make the hanger balance, nail them to the hanger. Hang the hanger over a hook. To weigh objects, place them in a paper cup and attach the cup to the clothespin. In this manner you can demonstrate the comparative weights of different objects, such as a cup of sawdust versus a cup of sugar. If you have lead weights, you can use these to find approximate weights of various objects.

The Principle of the Lever

Objective

To demonstrate the principle of the lever: increasing work without increasing effort.

Materials

A large board, a slat, two four-inch dowels, nails, a hammer, a wire, and a heavy object such as a battery.

Procedure

Nail the dowels upright on the end of the large board. Wrap the wire between the two dowels near the top. Have a child try to lift the heavy object from the table using the slat. Then have him place the slat over the wire, place the heavy object on the end of the slat and try to lift the object again by pushing down on the end of the slat. Your slat is a lever, and the wire is the fulcrum of that lever. Have several children try the lifting process, each time varying the length of the slat beyond the wire. Then have your class draw general conclusions about levers.

A Periscope

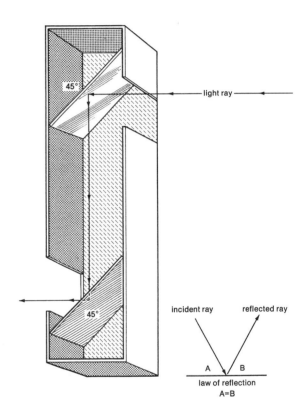

Objective

To demonstrate how light may be reflected.

Materials

Two small purse mirrors, a cardboard waxed paper box, a knife, and tape.

Procedure

Tape the mirrors in the box on a 45° angle, as is shown in the illustration. Cut slots in the side of the box so that you can look into the mirrors. Tape the box shut. To demonstrate the use of your periscope, shine a light into one mirror in a darkened room and observe how the light has been bent around. Draw a diagram of the reflection on the board and discuss with your class what is happening.

Pulleys

Objective

To demonstrate how a simple machine—the pulley—can increase work efficiency.

Materials

A wooden frame of 2 x 4 boards, two small pulleys, cuphooks, heavy cord or light rope, a hammer, six inches of doweling, and a weight.

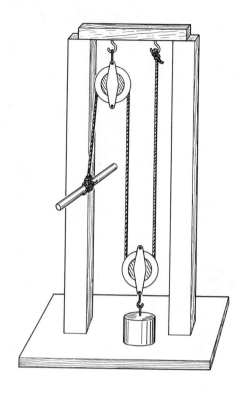

Procedure

Screw two cuphooks in the bottom of the top board about twelve inches apart. Hang a pulley from one hook and tie one end of the cord to the other hook. Thread the cord through the other pulley and then up through the fixed pulley. Tie the dowel on the end of the cord so it will not slip back through the pulley. Place a weight on the pulley that is hanging free. Using the dowel handle, pull the weight up and see how much effort it takes. Have several members of your class try to lift the weight by hand and then have them lift the weight using the pulley system. Let these students discuss their findings with the class.

Putting an Egg in a Bottle

Objective

To demonstrate that oxygen takes up space and that air expands when heated and contracts when cooled.

Materials

A hard-boiled egg, a milk bottle, a piece of paper, and matches.

Procedure

Shell a hard-boiled egg. Light a piece of paper with the match and drop it into the bottle. Set the egg on top of the bottle. When the air cools and contracts, it will pull the egg inside the bottle. Have your class discuss why this happened.

To get the egg out, wash the burned paper out of the bottle. Turn the bottle upside down and blow into it very hard. The egg should fly out of the bottle when you have blown a sufficient amount of air into the bottle. Be prepared to move the bottle away from your face quickly.

A Color Wheel

Objective

To demonstrate the principle of mixing colors as the eye perceives them.

Materials

A round of tagboard or cardboard, paints or crayons, a thread spool, a four-inch piece of thin doweling, and a cord.

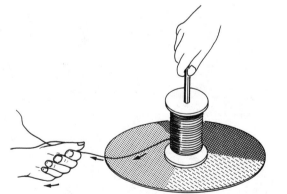

Procedure

Divide the round of tagboard into three equal sections and color them different colors. Glue the tagboard to the spool and insert the doweling into the hole. The spool should turn freely on the doweling. Wind the cord tightly around the spool. Turn the colored tagboard toward your class and pull the cord hard. Have your class comment on the color they see and why they see this color. Try the demonstration with other colors and see if your class can develop a general theory on mixing colors.

An Oxygen-Fire Experiment

Objective

To demonstrate that oxygen is necessary for a fire.

Materials

A six-inch candle, a pie pan, a match, water, and a glass.

Procedure

Light a candle and drip some wax into the pie pan. Blow out the candle and set it in the warm wax. Fill the pan three-fourths full with water. Light the candle again and place the glass over it. When the oxygen has been used up, the flame will go out and the water will be drawn up the glass. Discuss this with the members of your class and have them determine what has happened.

A Musical Instrument

Objective

To demonstrate a way in which different tones are produced by a stringed instrument.

Materials

A 1$^{\prime\prime}$ x 12$^{\prime\prime}$ x 2$^{\prime}$ board, a nail, a hammer, four feet of wire, a heavy object such as a rock or brick, and three small blocks of wood or three wooden clothespins.

Procedure

Hammer the nail into one end of the board. Tie one end of the wire to the nail and the other end to the heavy object. Drape

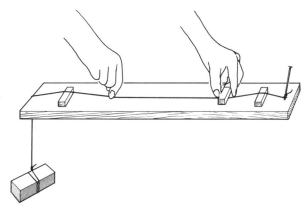

the wire along the board, allowing the object to hang free. Place the blocks of wood under the wire at different spots and pluck the wire. Have the class listen to the tone. Move the blocks and have the class listen again. Continue moving the blocks and plucking the wire until your class can decide a relationship exists between the length of the wire and the tone.

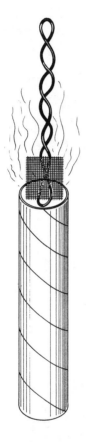

Making Sound with Hot Air

CAUTION: Be careful not to let the hot screen touch the sides of the tube.

Objective
To demonstrate that the motions of heat waves can produce sound.

Materials
A long cardboard mailing tube, six feet of baling wire, a square of galvanized wire screen, a Bunsen burner, a marking pen, and matches.

Procedure
Fold the baling wire in fourths and twist it together. Fold the wire screen in half and attach it to one end of the wire. Heat the screen until it turns red. When it is hot, lower it into the tube. The tube should be closed at the bottom. Gradually lower or raise the screen until you find the spot where as the screen cools it makes a wailing noise. Mark the spot where the noise occurs. Now you are ready to demonstrate this experiment to your class. Heat the screen again, lower it to your mark, and the wailing sound should be produced. Try this experiment with various sized tubes. Have members of your class explain what is happening to cause the sound.

9

A Quiz Board

Objective

To provide a stimulus for learning scientific facts during individual study periods.

Materials

A small sheet of pegboard, a large quantity of paper brads, bell or electrical wire, a battery, a very small socket and bulb, and small pictures and cards.

Procedure

Lay out your pegboard by estimating the number of pictures and questions you can fit on the front without cluttering it. You need a peghole in the center at the top of each picture. The pictures will all be on one side and the questions on the other. Do not attach the pictures or questions to the board yet. Push a paper brad into the hole above each picture and question and bend the fasteners back. Turn the board over and connect one picture brad to one question brad with the wire. Continue connecting two opposing brads in a random pattern until they are all connected. Screw the miniature socket onto the board. From one of the posts have a length of wire dangle down in the front; from the other post attach a wire to one of the battery posts. From the other battery post bring a wire through a hole to the front of your board and let it dangle as long as the other wire. The ends of the two dangling wires should be stripped of insulation, but make sure these wires are not connected to the battery when you strip them. Now attach the pictures and the questions or descriptions to the front of your board, making sure you place them in the spots that are wired together. If you can attach the cards, pictures, objects, or whatever you are using so that they can be removed and replaced, then you can change your quiz board periodically.

Set up your quiz board where your students can get to it without causing a disturbance. They should try to match the pictures on one side with the descriptions or questions on the other. If they think they have matched two correctly, they should press the end of one dangling wire to the brad above the picture and the end of the other wire to the brad above the description. If they are right, the light will go on.

You will find your quiz board an invaluable tool for interesting children in science and for providing an incentive to finish work.

Front view of a quiz board

	American elk	Whitetail deer	Mountain chickadee
	Grizzly bear	Eastern fox squirrel	Golden aster
	Wood duck	Mountain goat	Douglas fir
	Painted trillium	Killdeer	Pyrrhuloxia
	Catawba rhododendron	Bobwhite	Monarch butterfly

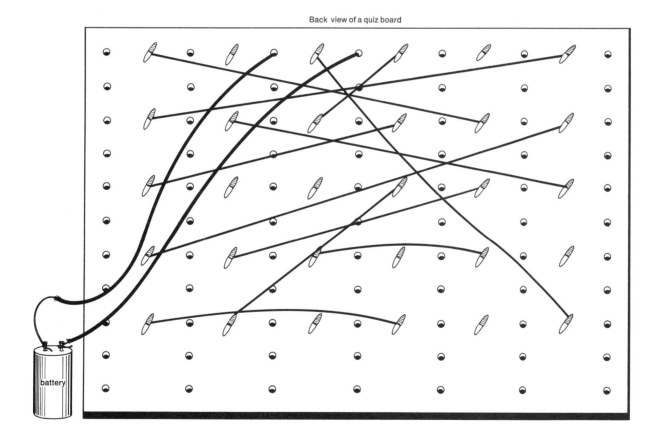

Back view of a quiz board